MY FRIEND has Dyspraxia

BY NICOLA EDWARDS

Chrysalis Education

Distributed in the United States by
Smart Apple Media
2140 Howard Drive West
North Mankato, Minnesota 56003

ISBN 1-59389-168-7 $25 J616.855 1/07

Library of Congress Control Number: 2004043613

Editorial Manager: Joyce Bentley
Editor: Jon Richards
Designer: Ben Ruocco
Photographer: Michael Wicks
Picture researcher: Lorna Ainger
Illustrations: Hardlines Ltd.

Produced by Tall Tree Ltd, U.K.

Consultant: Michele Lee, The Dyspraxia Foundation
The Dyspraxia Foundation is a charity which promotes awareness and understanding of dyspraxia and supports individuals and families affected by dyspraxia. To find out more about the charity, contact the office listed on page 31.

The photographer, author, and publishers would like to thank Sarah Ambler, Rosie Berkshire, Dylan Williams, Selwyn Williams, Aly Williams, Jon Whitehouse, Miles Gray, and Billy McHale for their help in preparing this book.

Picture acknowledgments:
Alamy/Kristjan Maack/Nordicphotos 29
Corbis/Lois Ellen Frank 21, Jeffry W Myers 24
Science Photo Library/Hattie Young 17, 28

Printed in China

Contents

*Words in **bold** are explained in the glossary on page 30.*

My friend Jamie

Jamie is happier now that he is getting help to deal with his dyspraxia.

Hello! My name's Mark and this is my friend Jamie. We're in the same class at school. We both belong to the same drama club, too, so we spend a lot of time together. Sometimes I feel a little shy in drama club when we have to make up a scene in a group, but Jamie doesn't. He wants to be an actor when he's older.

When Jamie first started coming to our school he didn't seem very happy. The teacher used to get angry with him for fidgeting and said he wasn't paying attention. He had problems in PE class, too. It used to take him too long to get ready and the teacher had to tie his shoes for him. Jamie used to get really fed up. Then he found out that he has **dyspraxia**. It's not an illness, but it does cause problems for him and he is getting help in dealing with them. He's getting along much better at school now. He even jokes about being dyspraxic. Maybe he'll become a comedian instead of an actor!

Jamie and Mark are good friends.
They make each other laugh.

DYSPRAXIA FACTS

DYSPRAXIA NUMBERS

Out of every 100 people, six are likely to be dyspraxic in some way. Three times more boys than girls are affected. The **symptoms** of dyspraxia vary from person to person, so no one experiences dyspraxia in exactly the same way.

What is dyspraxia?

Jamie can feel stressed when he has to write under time pressure, such as during a class test.

When Jamie was new in our class he seemed to struggle with the work we were doing. He had really messy handwriting and he found spelling to be difficult. He used to get disappointed when the teacher gave him low grades because his work wasn't neat. He used to forget a lot of things, too. We have PE on Tuesdays and Wednesdays and sometimes Jamie wouldn't be able to join in because he'd left his gym clothes at home.

Because of his dyspraxia, Jamie has to work hard to remember things. I try to help him at school. At the end of the day when we're packing up to go home, I remind him what homework we've been given and what books he needs to take home. But that's just to make sure—usually Jamie writes himself a note so that he doesn't forget.

Jamie makes a list to remind himself what homework he needs to do.

DYSPRAXIA FACTS

WHAT DOES IT MEAN?

Before dyspraxia was understood, it used to be called "Clumsy Child Syndrome." The word dyspraxia means "difficulty with movement" and comes from the Greek word for "doing" or "acting." Other names for dyspraxia include "Developmental **Coordination** Disorder" and "Motor Learning Difficulties" (motor means movement).

Different every day

Mr. Eliott helps Jamie in class by making sure that Jamie understands clearly any instructions.

At breaktime, Jamie and I go to the playground with our friends. Jamie's got lots of friends now, but when he started school things were different. Some kids in our class used to tease him and call him names. They made fun of him because he had problems getting dressed for PE. Sometimes he'd come back into class with his shoes on the wrong feet and they'd laugh at him.

Mr. Eliott used to get frustrated with Jamie when he forgot to bring in his homework. Jamie remembers how Mr. Eliott would explain something to the class one day, and the next day Jamie would have forgotten all about it. "I couldn't explain what was going on in my head," Jamie says. "It used to upset me that people thought I was useless at everything. Once everyone found out about my dyspraxia they were much more friendly."

With the help of his teachers and friends, Jamie is much more confident in class.

DYSPRAXIA FACTS

THE HIDDEN HANDICAP

Dyspraxia is often described as the "hidden handicap" because it's impossible to tell by looking at someone whether or not they have dyspraxia. Dyspraxia affects a lot of people. In a class of 30 children, at least one of them is likely to be dyspraxic. It helps dyspraxic children if the people around them understand what dyspraxia is and how it affects the people who have it.

What causes dyspraxia?

When you catch a ball, signals from your eyes are sent through nerves to your brain, which then sends signals to your muscles.

No one knows exactly what causes dyspraxia. Experts believe that it might have something to do with the way in which the brain sends information through the **nervous system** to the rest of the body. Scientists have shown that the brains of people with dyspraxia are not damaged, but that the nerves which carry information from the brain may be slower to develop than in other people.

The brain receives information from the body's senses, then it processes the information and sends signals back to the body, instructing it how to react as a result of the information. Messages to and from the brain are carried by the nerves. If the nerves haven't developed properly, the signals may become mixed up and unclear.

If there are confused signals traveling between the brain and the body, it may be difficult to make sense of the information being received and

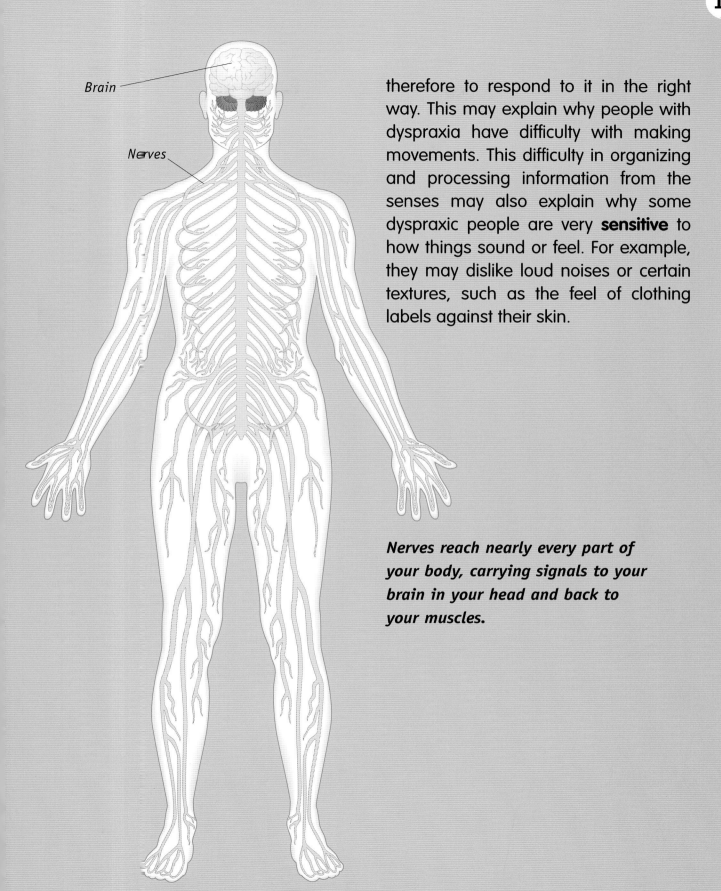

Brain

Nerves

therefore to respond to it in the right way. This may explain why people with dyspraxia have difficulty with making movements. This difficulty in organizing and processing information from the senses may also explain why some dyspraxic people are very **sensitive** to how things sound or feel. For example, they may dislike loud noises or certain textures, such as the feel of clothing labels against their skin.

Nerves reach nearly every part of your body, carrying signals to your brain in your head and back to your muscles.

Jamie's little sister

Jamie and Mark have brought a birthday present for Jamie's sister, Megan.

Jamie has a little sister named Megan. She's going to be two years old this week. Megan loves those toys where you have to put a shape through the matching hole. At first, she would just bang the toy with any shapes. But then we showed her where each shape was meant to go. Now she can push the different shapes through the holes all by herself.

Jamie's mom says Megan is learning how each shape fits into the right hole. She uses her brain to plan what she is going to do and judges the movements she needs to make so the shape goes through the correct hole. Then her brain sends signals to the muscles in her body to tell them what to do. Megan's brain does this automatically, and it all happens so quickly! Jamie says his sister's much better at those kinds of puzzles than he was when he was the same age. His mom explained that this was probably because of his dyspraxia.

Jamie's sister, Megan, likes to play with a shape puzzle like this one.

DYSPRAXIA FACTS

SPOTTING DYSPRAXIA

Dyspraxia can be **diagnosed** at any age, but the earlier it is recognized the better, so that children can be helped as soon as possible. Some early signs of possible dyspraxia include:

- as a baby, being slow to start crawling or preferring "bottom shuffling" to crawling
- being slow to start talking
- as a young child, taking a long time to get dressed and consistently putting shoes on the wrong feet
- being very forgetful
- being a messy eater and finding it difficult to use cutlery

Diagnosing dyspraxia

After seeing that Jamie was having trouble with his school work, Mr. Eliott suggested it might help Jamie to see an educational psychologist.

"What made you think I might be dyspraxic, Mom?" Jamie asked one day. "Well," said Jamie's mom, "you didn't seem to be settling in well at school. Sometimes you didn't want to go in at all, especially if it was a day when you had PE. Your teacher was worried about how you were doing, too. He told us that you were having problems with writing and with math. And we didn't understand why you kept forgetting things and found it so difficult to

The tests that Jamie did with Mr. Briggs showed that Jamie has dyspraxia.

be organized. Dad and I went to see Dr. Cassidy, our doctor, and she suggested that we take you to see Mr. Briggs, who is an **educational psychologist**."

Jamie remembers going to see Mr. Briggs. He says that Mr. Briggs went through some tests with him. "Afterward, Mr. Briggs called Mom and Dad back in," remembers Jamie. "He said he had found out that I was dyspraxic and that I was also very bright. That was wonderful! Nobody had ever told me that before!"

DYSPRAXIA FACTS

BRIGHT CHILDREN

Dyspraxia has nothing to do with low intelligence—dyspraxic children are often very bright but have trouble showing others just how much they know. There are lots of ways in which children can overcome the problems that their dyspraxia causes them.

Treating dyspraxia

Jamie now uses graph paper for his school work. It helps him to organize his math and writing.

Mr. Briggs explained to Jamie and his parents that no two people with dyspraxia experience exactly the same symptoms, so Jamie's form of dyspraxia was unique to him. He said that there were different people who could help Jamie deal with the problems his dyspraxia was causing him. "One of these therapists is Mrs. Phillips," Jamie told me. "Mom told me she's a **developmental optometrist**. Remember how I used to have problems

G 15 2008

SEP 0 9 2008

SEP 2 7 2008

NOV 0 4 2008

NOV 2 0 2008

DEC 0 5 2008

DEC 1 0 2008

JAN 1 4 2009

MAR 1 4 2009

2

FEB 0 3 2009
JAN 2 6 2009

JAN 2 1 2009

JAN 1 7 2009

PLEASE KEEP THIS CARD IN THE BOOK POCKET.
THIS BOOK IS DUE ON THE LATEST DATE STAMPED.

PLEASE KEEP THIS CARD IN THE BOOK POCKET.
THIS BOOK IS DUE ON THE LATEST DATE STAMPED.

Children with dyspraxia can also be treated by a speech therapist, who can help them to speak more clearly. Other therapists include physiotherapists and occupational therapists.

copying from the board in class? Mrs. Phillips said it's because my eyes have difficulty **tracking** what's written on the board. She's given me exercises to do with my eyes, which have made them work much better."

Sometimes simple things can make a big difference. For math, instead of lined paper, Mr. Eliott gives Jamie graph paper, so that he can organize how he writes his work better. "My work's much neater now," Jamie says.

DYSPRAXIA FACTS

UNDERSTANDING DYSPRAXIA

Dyspraxia is not an illness, so there's no "cure" for it. However, there are lots of ways to deal with the effects of dyspraxia and being dyspraxic doesn't have to stop anyone from achieving anything. It can be useful to talk about having dyspraxia and help other people to understand its effects.

Ready for school

Jamie lays out his clothes for the next day.

Every morning, I pick up Jamie on the way to school and we walk there together. Before Jamie's dyspraxia was diagnosed, he often wasn't ready when I arrived at his house. Now he's much more organized. Jamie says: "Mr. Briggs suggested that, before I go to bed at night, I put out all the clothes I want to wear in the morning. I lay them over the back of a chair in the order I'm going to put them on." Jamie's shoes have velcro fastenings so he doesn't have to worry about tying laces. "Luckily, I don't have to wear shirts with buttons for school, since they can be difficult to button," Jamie explains.

Before he leaves the house, Jamie checks the notes he's stuck on the back of the front door to remind him what he needs to take to school. As we leave, Jamie clips his front door key to the waistband of his pants, so that he doesn't lose it.

Before Jamie leaves home, he remembers to check everything that he needs to take to school.

DYSPRAXIA FACTS

SENSITIVE FEELINGS

Some dyspraxic children can take a strong dislike to the feel of certain things, such as the sensation of their hair being brushed or cut, or the feel of a toothbrush in their mouth. Some dyspraxic children say it has helped them to use an electric toothbrush instead.

Meal times

Jamie likes to choose what he takes to school for his lunch.

Lunch times at school used to be a real problem for Jamie. "I used to find it hard to carry a tray with a plate of food on it, and I used to hate some of the food they served, especially mashed potato." Jamie also found it difficult to use a knife and fork and the lunchroom staff used to scold him for

When Jamie comes to my house we often have pizza to eat. It's easier for Jamie if he doesn't have to use cutlery.

making a mess. "I never wanted to pour myself some water, either," Jamie remembers, "because I was scared that I might spill it all over the place."

Things are better now that Jamie brings his lunch to school. He only brings in things that he can eat with his fingers. He has a carton of juice every day and he uses a straw to drink it so that it doesn't spill if he knocks it over. Lots of us pack our lunch too, and we all sit together.

DYSPRAXIA FACTS

FOOD DISLIKES

Like Jamie, some dyspraxic children may have a strong dislike for the feel and texture of certain foods in their mouths, such as mashed potatoes. It helps them if people understand this aspect of their dyspraxia and don't give them foods they dislike.

In the classroom

Now that he is getting help with his dyspraxia, Jamie is much happier in school. In his report, Mr. Briggs made lots of suggestions. He said that the way Jamie sits when he is writing is really important. Now Jamie sits upright on his chair with both his feet flat on the floor. We are allowed to do our homework on a computer, if we have one at home. Jamie says he likes using the computer to present his ideas in different ways.

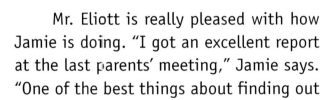

Opposite: **Jamie sits at the front of the class, so that he can hear the teacher clearly and doesn't get distracted.**

Jamie uses a computer to help organize his homework and home life.

Mr. Eliott is really pleased with how Jamie is doing. "I got an excellent report at the last parents' meeting," Jamie says. "One of the best things about finding out that I have dyspraxia was being told I'm smart," Jamie told me. "Before, when I used to get things wrong all the time, I used to think I was stupid."

DYSPRAXIA FACTS

COPING WITH DYSPRAXIA

Using a computer can help children with dyspraxia to organize their ideas and gives them a break from having to concentrate on their handwriting. Other ways of being organized include labeling things needed for school, such as a pencil case or lunchbox, storing things in labeled containers, and using a bulletin board at home for reminders. Children can also use different pen and pencil grips and sloping boards to write on in class.

On the playground

When Jamie first came to our school, he used to stand on his own in the playground. We thought he was shy, but now we know it was because he was worried that people would laugh at him. Jamie also didn't think we'd want him to join in, because he used to find PE really difficult. "It isn't just that I find it difficult to get changed, I also find throwing and catching a ball tricky and someone said I run in a funny way. I suppose it's because I move my arms more than other people when I run."

Jamie has had some **physiotherapy** to help him with some of the problems caused by his dyspraxia. He has been given exercises to do to build up the strength in his muscles and to improve his coordination. Jamie has to practice these exercises at home, but he says they're fun to do so he doesn't mind.

Opposite: **Children with dyspraxia may worry about walking through or playing in a crowd, because they might bump into and annoy people.**

Jamie enjoys playing soccer with his friends.

DYSPRAXIA FACTS

PHYSICAL PROBLEMS

Children who are dyspraxic may find it difficult to stand on one leg, hop, or jump. Some may struggle to learn to ride a bike, or to throw and catch a ball. But physiotherapy and practice can help. There are many sports which dyspraxic children can enjoy and which can help them to develop their coordination skills. These include swimming, tennis, soccer, golf, climbing, rowing, and horseback riding.

At drama club

On Tuesdays after school, Jamie and I go to our local drama club. Jamie thinks it's great. "My favorite part is when we do an **improvisation**. That means we act in a group and just say what comes into our heads. We don't have to remember any lines and there are no right or wrong answers! It feels really good when we're all acting together and the teacher says we did well."

Opposite: **Jamie really enjoys dressing up and acting. He would like to be an actor when he's older.**

Jamie and Mark are now close friends and have lots of fun doing many different activities.

We've met lots of new people at the drama group and made friends with them. Next month we're going to put on a show for our parents. Jamie's helping to design the show's posters because he's really good at art.

Sometimes we have to act on our own. That can be scary, but Jamie seems to enjoy making speeches. He says: "It's great to go to drama group if I'm angry about something. I can act out how I'm feeling and that makes me feel better!"

DYSPRAXIA FACTS

FEELING CONFIDENT

It's important that children with dyspraxia know that it's not their fault and that it's nothing to be ashamed of—it's part of what makes them who they are. Feeling confident and knowing that there are things they are good at can help them to overcome the difficulties caused by their dyspraxia.

Questions people ask

Q. **Who gets dyspraxia?**
A. Dyspraxia isn't a disease like measles that anyone can "catch." No one knows exactly what causes dyspraxia, but experts think it has something to do with the development of the nerves that pass information and instructions to and from the brain (see pages 10–11). Dyspraxia can result from the way in which a child's brain and nervous system develops, or it can occur later as the result of illness or injury to the brain.

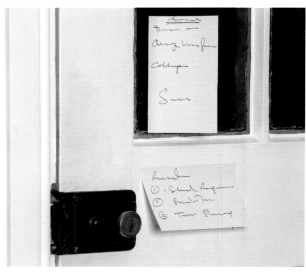

Writing lists and leaving reminders can help people with dyspraxia.

Children can learn how to cope with dyspraxia with the help of speech therapists and other professionals.

Q. **Is there a cure for dyspraxia?**
A. Dyspraxia isn't an illness, so there isn't a "cure" for it and it's not possible to "grow out of" being dyspraxic. However, there are many ways of dealing with the problems that dyspraxia can cause, and being dyspraxic doesn't have to stop anyone from achieving whatever they want to achieve.

Q. **How can I tell if I'm dyspraxic?**
A. No two people experience dyspraxia in exactly the same way and each dyspraxic person has a variety of different symptoms. These symptoms may include difficulties with speech,

throwing, catching or kicking a ball, getting dressed and tying shoelaces, and problems with handwriting and math. If you think you may have some symptoms of dyspraxia, talk to someone you trust at home or at school.

Q. What's it like to be dyspraxic?
A. Being dyspraxic can be very frustrating and isolating. It's hard to struggle with things that other people seem to find straightforward, such as getting dressed for PE at school. Dyspraxic children can worry about their school work and feel unhappy if their grades aren't as good as others in the class. It can make them feel anxious and lacking in confidence. Sometimes they may not want to go to school at all. Children with dyspraxia feel happier when people are understanding about their difficulties and offer them support and encouragement to work hard in order to overcome them.

Q. How can I help my friend who is dyspraxic?
A. Find out all you can about dyspraxia and try to understand the difficulties that people with dyspraxia can experience. Sometimes, dyspraxic children have been bullied by people who don't understand dyspraxia, which makes them feel very sad and lonely. If you know someone who is

Children with dyspraxia can enjoy taking part in sports, including swimming.

being bullied, let them know you're their friend and that you don't agree with the bullies. Tell a teacher or someone else you trust about the bullying, so that it can be stopped. You can help your friend with dyspraxia by encouraging them to join in with things at school and by helping them when they need it, for example, by checking that they know what they need to take home for homework.

Glossary

coordination The organization of the body's movements so that they work together in a smooth and balanced way.

developmental optometrist Someone who has studied how children's eyes develop and who can help children who are having problems with their eyesight.

diagnose To identify a problem such as dyspraxia by looking at someone's symptoms and the results of tests carried out on them.

dyspraxia A collection of symptoms showing that someone has difficulty with organizing their movements, which may lead to problems with speech, handwriting, math, getting dressed, and physical coordination.

educational psychologist Someone who has studied how children learn and can help children who are having difficulty with their school work.

improvisation Making up an acting performance "on the spot" rather than following a script.

muscles Fibers in the body that can become shorter and then longer again to allow movement of body parts, such as the arms and the legs.

nerves Bundles of thin, threadlike fibers in the body that pass messages to and from the brain.

nervous system The network of nerves that allows messages to be carried between the brain and every part of the body.

occupational therapist A qualified person who helps others to overcome or deal with physical or social problems by showing them activities that they can take part in.

physiotherapy A form of treatment that uses exercises to improve muscles and strength as well as coordination.

sensitive Being very aware of or irritated by the sensation of something such as a certain texture, temperature, smell, or noise.

speech therapist Someone who has studied how a person speaks and can help people to speak more clearly and improve their communication skills.

symptoms The ways in which someone shows that they may have a particular problem or illness; for example, coughs, sneezes, and a sore throat are symptoms of a cold.

tracking When referring to the eyes, tracking describes the movements that a person's eyes make to enable them to read some text or take in information from a picture.

Useful organizations

HERE ARE SOME ORGANIZATIONS YOU MIGHT LIKE TO CONTACT FOR MORE INFORMATION ABOUT DYSPRAXIA

AMERICAN SPEECH-LANGUAGE-HEARING ASSOCIATION (ASHA)
10801 Rockville Pike
Rockville, MD 20852-3279
Tel: 301 987 5700
Fax: 301 571 0457
Email: actioncenter@asha.org
www.asha.org

LEARNING DISABILITIES ASSOCIATION OF AMERICA
4256 Library Road
Pittsburgh, PA 15234-1349
Tel: 412 341 1515
Fax: 412 344 0224
www.ldanatl.org

THE DYSPRAXIA FOUNDATION
8 West Alley
Hitchin
Herts SG5 1EG
UK
Tel: +44 1462 454986/455016
www.dyspraxiafoundation.org.uk

THERAPY IN PRAXIS LIMITED
P.O. Box 90
Kirkbymoorside
York YO62 6YE
UK
www.therapyinpraxisltd.co.uk

OTHER WEBSITES

www.matts-hideout.co.uk
Not an organization, but a very useful website run by teenager Matthew Alden-Farrow. On the site, Matt talks about his experience of being dyspraxic and explains how he deals with his dyspraxia.

Index